What the *!! *!! is Fit ANYWAY?

ANDREA SEXTON

Cover image by: The Dream Loft
Book design by: SWATT Books Ltd

Printed in the United Kingdom
First Printing, 2021

ISBN: 978-1-8383948-0-6 (Paperback)
ISBN: 978-1-8383948-1-3 (eBook)

Admire PR
2 Old Clothiers Arms, Market Street,
Nailsworth, Gloucestershire , GL6 0BX

www.admire-pr.com

Contents

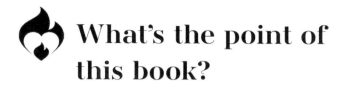

What's the point of this book?

Let's get straight down to it....

This book is an introduction to PR. It won't answer all your questions, nor is it likely to turn you into an overnight celebrity success (sorry about that). It will give you a good basis to start with and will help you ask the right questions when you are looking for a great PR to work with.

I take a slightly different view of PR than many other industry professionals. Much what I do stretches into the traditional marketing space due to my sales and strategy background. Too many people when they think of PR, think only of press releases and getting into the press as editorial. While that is a huge part of what a PR person does it's not the whole story.

My favourite definition of PR is:

Public Relations professionals help a business or individual **cultivate a positive reputation** with the public through various unpaid or earned communications, including traditional media, social media, and in-person engagements.

They also help clients **defend their reputation during a crisis** that threatens their credibility.

PR Myths

I asked some business people what PR means to them and got some brilliant answers...

"How others perceive myself and my company, through others word of mouth"

"The coordinated effort to affect public perception"

"Letting people know what your business does"

"PR to means proactive 'good news' output to either promote subtlety or combat negative press with a view to increasing awareness"

"A way to make good businesses more visible via clever mediums for success stories or notable wins"

"Public awareness of what you do, have done, or are going to be doing"

"The promotion of news surrounding a person or a business – sometimes good and sometimes not so good"

"A form of marketing"

"Getting exposure of your message for 'free' via existing media channels that are looking for interesting, topical stories that you can help create or piggyback onto"

What is interesting is everyone said something slightly different – and yet they are all correct.

To me this is the essence:

PR is building and guarding your positive public reputation – as a brand, a business, or as a business person.

I also believe...

EVERYTHING YOU SAY AND DO IS PR (AT ALL TIMES!)

PR is not complicated but it takes effort and persistence. As PRs, We light the fire and keep it burning. Public relations is a deliberate and carefully thought out process and It requires ongoing and sustained activity.

Part 1:

Setting the scene and getting started

It's time to get your pens. Make notes as you go through this book – writing stuff down can help this process. It really helps if you can take some time out of your schedule to have a think about this first part of the book in a relaxed space. Ideas will come to you more readily when you are in a calm frame of mind. This is why often people say they have their greatest business ideas early in the morning or as they drift off to sleep.

Your Business

We need to start by thinking about your business AND yourself as a business person. This will help you know what your key messages are for all your marketing and communication to your staff and your customers.

Start with these 5 questions.

- **WHY** do you get up in the morning and do what you do? And Why are you different as a business?

- **VISION** A depiction of where you want the company to be in 5 to 10 years and the impact you intend to leave on customers

- **MISSION** A declaration of your business strategy that supports the vision statement

- **VALUES** Core principles of the company

- **CULTURE** The collective personality your whole team displays to each other and to customers and the greater community

Values guide decision-making and a sense of what's important and what's right. A company's values should never change as they are the foundation that will be there in 10, 20 or even 100 years from now. They are the uncompromising core principles that the company is willing to live and die by. The rules of the game.

Culture is the current embodiment of the values as the needs of the business dictate. The benefits of corporate culture are both common sense and supported by social science. It has been stated that culture can account for 20-30% of the differential in corporate performance when compared with culturally unremarkable competitors.

To help you these are the ones for my company, Admire PR.

Why

I started Admire as I love promotion and helping other companies and individuals shine in a way that is true to them. I like to be in the background – like a cheerleader in support of their efforts – steering them to success and to achieve their goals. We price fairly for the work we do, monitor all results and always have a plan B.

Vision

To build an ethical company that guards and builds the brands of our clients with pure transparency and excellence at all times.

Mission

To dispel the myths of PR and make excellent public relations accessible and relevant to all business people and companies. Our clients reputation is of utmost importance to us. We are clear and transparent and set aspirational objectives and KPIs that we achieve.

We do all the basic work brilliantly and this allows us to add extra value with creative and bold work.

Values

We are:

- Curious – we are always learning
- Tenacious – we never, ever give up
- Creative – we always have a plan B
- Intentional – deliberate and carefully thought out actions

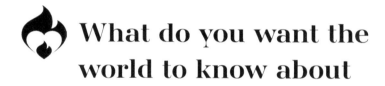 What do you want the world to know about

Write down any aspects of your business that you need to promote – these can be products, brands, people, events – anything you want the rest of the world to know about. Write it all down in any order at first.

When you have written it all down you can think about a priority order depending on your business strategy over the year and what needs to be promoted each quarter.

Keep your list handy. As business events and opportunities crop up you can add them into your list as time goes on. This list will help you decide where PR can help you.

# Your Customers

Now let's think about your customers – who are your current customers – are they the right ones? Are there other people you want to reach? Who are they?

Some people use Avatars and give their ideal customers names and identities. This can help in big teams or if you are a visual thinker – so you can give your customer avatars names and draw pictures of them.

I tend to divide my customers depending on the industry sector initially then divide it down into customer characteristics. Some companies can divide initially on target job titles.

Questions to ask include...

- Where did they come from? (current customers)
- Who are they?
- Where do they live ?
- What are they interested in?
- What do they read?
- What do they watch on TV?
- What social channels do they use?
- Where do they work? Do they travel for work?

I love this bit. This is where you need to think about how you can reach people with information about your business and products.

You need to think a bit laterally.

I once held a PR strategy workshop with a client, and we realised that the customer they were trying to reach had a common mentality rather than a common job title. We realised their ideal client would be curious about learning certain things, so we started looking for events they would potentially be at.

For example for you could be if CEOs of financial service firms in London are your targets then thinking about what they might read on the commute into work is a good starting point. Then think about other ways to reach your audience. What about travel? What magazines are available in the executive lounges at airports?

Marketing and PR – Where does it all fit?

One of the questions I'm asked most often is what the difference between marketing and PR. PR is part of marketing; one of the tools you can use to market your business or product.

Marketing has countless definitions. In basic terms, it is the process through which products and services move from idea to the customer. It includes identification of a product/service, determining demand, deciding on its price, and selecting distribution channels. It also includes developing and implementing a promotional strategy.

I always tell people to think of the promotional part of their marketing as a chocolate orange and each of the segments are the activities you will undertake to promote your product or service.

These can segments include:

PR activities including:

- Editorial – news and opinion
- Product reviews
- Speaking opportunities
- Brand ambassadors / Influencers
- Sponsorship
- Broadcast – TV and Radio

- Networking
- Awards

Wider marketing activities including:

- Website
- Blogs
- Social Media
- Advertising
- Advertorial
- Emails
- Brochures
- Catalogues
- Direct mail (stuff in the post)
- Events
- Telemarketing

Have a look at these main PR and marketing tools and decide which is most appropriate for reaching your customers. You will potentially need to test things out and measure the results to discover the best approach.

Even if I am looking after just one aspect of PR for a client – all the others marketing activities they are undertaking need considering. Everything must work together. As a PR it's important for me to work with all the marketing functions of a business. Often there is a social media manager and a marketing manager in place when I become involved as part of a team. The key is to communicate between us and to integrate all the activities to make the most of all the promotional opportunities.

Part 2:

Getting Into
the Press

Let's be honest – this is what the PR bread and butter is and this is what I spend the majority of my time doing. When I'm thinking of the press I'm talking about newspapers, magazines, TV, radio, blogs, podcasts and both on and offline. What follows are a few of the best ways that I use with clients to help them gain press coverage.

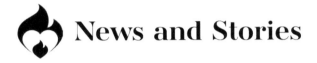 News and Stories

Decide what media you want to get into. Buy a copy or read it online and check out what sections they have and what sorts of stories get printed. If it's radio or TV then watch it or listen to it.

You need a story or a hook – that is appealing. You need a second opinion as what you find interesting probably isn't to the rest of the world – sorry about that but it's true!

Journalists have tight deadlines. The best thing to do is to call the publication and find out who you need to contact and how they like to be contacted. Many journalists prefer emails and probably won't appreciate you harassing them to see if they got your information – though I bet if there are journalists reading this they will be laughing as they know I do this sometimes :-)

When you email, make it brief and to the point. Include all info within the email body if possible and don't attach huge files. I'm a fan of less is more. You can send a press release – I will come on to what that should look like. Do not attach PDFs and do not put images within the text. Make life easy for the journalist.

Company and people news is good – genuine charity stories or amazing things your staff or clients are doing are also good. New products, new staff, new facilities, events and awards are also great topics. Think outside of what you do as a business and look at what is going on in the community and what you can get involved in. Be current and topical. Bear in mind that if there is a huge national story it may be harder to get your news into the press.

New Product Launches

S tart with what customers you need to see the product and where you can reach them (what they will read or look at)

New products are interesting and are generally one of the easiest things to get coverage on. As long as the product is great quality and works well there is no reason why it shouldn't get featured. The warning here is that it will take some time to gain traction. Magazines will need to wait until there is space so be patient and start to plan well ahead. It can take 4-6 months for products to be featured

Send a short info about the product (50 words is fine – unless you are asked for more), RRP, where it can be bought from and an appropriate sized image for the media. Print media will need high res images – its good to have both cut out product images and lifestyle images available

Bloggers and magazines will often review new products so make sure you have allocated a number of samples for review

Competitions and Giveaways

D o you have the budget to give something away or hold a competition? This is a good way to get both in print or on an online publication. It's also a valuable way to create links to your social media. In general the amount of editorial you receive will depend upon the value of the prize.

The Press Release

The Press Release is a way of packaging information in an easy to read manner for journalists.

There is a way that I prefer to lay out the information so that journalists have everything they need.

Include:

- Date it can be released.
- A quote.
- A link or a call to action

Here is an example of one of mine for a bike shop. It was for news sections of the local and cycling press so needed to be less than 150 words.

For Immediate Release:

Chris Boardman opens Bike Science Bristol

British cycling legend Chris Boardman was on hand to open the new Bike Science Bristol shop on Whiteladies Road. He spent several hours discussing cycling and the Boardman range of bikes with over one hundred Bike Science customers.

"We are delighted with our new premises and that Chris could come and officially open the shop. We have bikes to suit all levels of cyclist and you can be sure to get the perfect bike for your needs as well as exceptional after-purchase support" Andy Sexton, Director of Bike Science.

Bike Science offer bikes from both the Elite and Performance Boardman range, Kuota, Van Nicholas and Legend. Bike Fitting using Retul 3D Motion Capture Technology, Performance testing, Physiotherapy and full workshop facilities are available alongside bike accessories and clothing.

Visit: www.bike-science.com for further details.

//:ENDS

Press contact: Andrea Sexton
Email and Phone Number

At this point you can add some additional notes for the editors with company information and any other links you think will be useful

Example 2 – this is a longer release that has information about more than one company. I had 2 clients working together with Gloucester Rugby.

For Immediate Release

World Leading Digital Technology at Gloucester Rugby

A groundbreaking partnership between digital infrastructure specialists Landways, digital agency Clock, and Gloucester Rugby will bring a new generation of digital services to the Gloucester stadium.

Landways is expert in next-generation digital infrastructure and is focussed on high-density venues including sports stadiums.

Landways has designed, financed and built an industry-leading high density digital infrastructure and Wi-Fi network at Kingsholm Stadium. The infrastructure is completely future-proofed and will cope with several generations of data growth, network upgrades and new digital services.

Chris Smedley, Chief Executive of Landways, said:

"We have deployed a record quantity of optical fibre throughout the stadium, as well as several unique technical designs, to manage the huge forecast growth in demand for wireless data over the next few years. We will be monitoring the network closely and, as required, working with Gloucester Rugby to install upgrades to ensure that the Wi-Fi system does not run out of capacity and that Kingsholm remains one of the UK's best-connected sports venues."

This state-of-the-art capacity will underpin a new generation of digital services to be provided to Gloucester Rugby by digital agency Clock. A new fan experience mobile app will use Clock's Colooder platform to deliver a variety of experiences including half-time quizzes, games that allow children to interact, play and understand the game of rugby, a range of audio feeds to enhance what's going on in the game, pre-ordering of food & drinks, rewards & offers, debates and discussions, live Man of the Match voting, a fans' gallery of pictures and exclusive content around players, the game and fans.

The partnership of Clock with Landways is heaven sent. The richer experiences Clock will deliver are not possible in most stadiums because the connectivity and Wi-Fi are poor. Landways expertise in infrastructure means there is a fibre network that will allow multiple audio and video streams to be delivered live, connected screens and access, and connected food, drink and merchandise. As part of the fan experience platform, clubs will be able to offer forward thinking brands many more opportunities than traditional rights holder or sponsor relationships

Ben Silcox, Chief Strategy Officer of Clock, said:

"We are excited to be bringing to life Gloucester Rugby's vision for a truly connected stadium and mobile app to make the fan experience easier, richer and more unique than any other rugby club. Landways and Clock are investing heavily in this project as a sign of their commitment and belief that Gloucester Rugby fans will benefit from a world-class experience."

Stephen Vaughan, Gloucester Rugby CEO commented:

"We are firmly in a digital world and part of the 'future proofing' of the club going forward is to ensure we are at the forefront of technology that allows us to give everybody that visits Kingsholm stadium not only fast connectivity but also gives us the ability to engage our audiences better. The app will allow visitors to Kingsholm to access high speed Wi-fi and a range of services designed to improve the experience on a match day. We are delighted to be partnering with both Landways and Clock to help provide a more connected environment for our fans."

Ben Silox commented "The future is looking bright for our partnership with Landways. There are too many clubs and venues not delivering experiences that people have come to expect in other parts of their lives; the sum of the technology is not adding up to something better. With our unique partnership of a connected infrastructure and an end to end connected fan experience, we are well positioned to help rights holders and venues gain commercial growth and a younger fan and customer base. Our rugby clients are moving first but we are experiencing interest across a range of sports and live experience venues."

//: ENDS

Editors Notes:

About Gloucester Rugby

Formed in 1873, Gloucester Rugby are a professional rugby union club who, in 2018-19, will compete in the Gallagher Premiership, the European Rugby Champions Cup and the Anglo-Welsh Cup.

Over 120 Gloucester Rugby players have played international rugby and the team management is currently headed up by Director of Rugby David Humphreys, who is a former Ireland international and Head Coach Johan Ackermann, a former Springbok.

The club has won the domestic cup competition on five separate occasions and the European Rugby Challenge Cup twice.

Kingsholm in recent seasons has established itself as a regular venue for international as well as club rugby. The stadium hosted four matches in the Rugby World Cup 2015 and has also hosted the likes of Barbarians, Australia, Ireland, Japan, Samoa, Tonga, Fiji and Georgia.

The club has also developed a reputation for hosting live music concerts during the close season. Since May 2011, when The Wanted became the first band to perform live at Kingsholm, the stadium has hosted concerts by the likes of Elton John, Jess Glynne, McFly, Lionel Richie and Madness. Sir Tom Jones has even played at Kingsholm on two separate occasions! However, the biggest concert held at the stadium was in June 2017 when Little Mix attracted a crowd of 19,000.

About Landways (www.landways.com)

Landways is a specialist in the design, build, financing and operation of next generation integrated digital infrastructure for high density in-building environments, based upon strong long-term relationships with site-owners to help deliver their objectives in a digital world.

Formed in 2017 by former senior managers from Geo Networks and backed by US internet infrastructure investors, Columbia Capital, Landways offers a range of Infrastructure as a Service (IaaS) solutions to help its customers make the transition to a "Wireless First" access model, supporting very high levels of concurrent device usage and best in class service levels.

Through the design, build, financing and operation of digital infrastructure, Landways delivers future-proofed optical fibre-based networks that grow and evolve to support the ever-increasing use of data by users in high density environments, where digital coverage is often poor. Its designs avoid the need to rip out and replace legacy systems, thus saving significant sums for its customers.

Further, Landways' data and power infrastructure designs are capable of being extended to provide highly efficient ways of integrating other parallel and synergistic areas of in-building technical facilities management, such as LED lighting upgrades, audio systems, digital signage connectivity, CCTV, security, smart monitoring, building management, power generation and storage.

Landways adopts an open access model enabling multiple service providers to use its wireless infrastructure, thus allowing access for third party providers including mobile networks and other digital operators to launch new and innovative products and services to all users within the venue.

Landways works closely with its customers' chosen partners to ensure that the best possible use is made of its enabling digital infrastructure to deliver a variety of innovative new digital services to customers and visitors, allowing these locations to be at the forefront of the new generation of highly connected venues.

About Clock (www.clock.co.uk)

Clock has delivered uniquely valuable experiences for clients for over 20 years. Our clients typically need to bridge the physical and digital in order to find new growth. We design, build, engineer and execute digital products and services across the customer experience.

Clock was founded in 1997 with a grant from the Prince's Trust, pioneering many of the first applications of digital technology into brand experiences and communications. Since then Clock have worked with a range of clients across sectors that include publishing, media, retail, hospitality, betting, sports, eSports and electronic games; awarded many times over the past decade, most recently for work with Leicester Tigers.

Clock provides consultancy and project delivery as well as investment into collaborative long term partnerships. By aligning strategic, delivery and commercial goals with a long history of expertise in deploying technology and customer experience solutions – we are able to help with the messiness of everyday business.

 Becoming an Expert

If I ask most people what they are expert at they often say 'nothing'. But I bet that isn't true.

Answer these questions.

- What do you love doing? What is your 'thing' (this does not need to be business related by the way – you can still promote you and your business on the back of something totally unrelated).

- What are you amazing at?

- What knowledge do you have that few other people have?

- Where can you share this knowledge? This could be the local paper, a blog, a guest blog, LinkedIn, a video or as an article in a trade publication.

Blogging and Guest Blogging

You may already have a blog – how well do you use it? People are often afraid of sharing their knowledge in case someone 'steals' it. Don't fret – I totally believe in give and get. If you can give some knowledge, it cements your standing as one of the best in your business. I'm not a weekly blogger myself – I'm too busy writing clients blogs – but I do regularly update my own blog.

Writing a guest blog is an excellent way to share your knowledge online and on social media. A few LinkedIn shares can work wonders for you.

Write a list of blogs you admire and see if they take guest opinions.

If you want some ideas about where you can guest blog then do contact me on social media and I will have a think for you.

If you are not a confident writer consider having someone write for you. It's worth spending a little on this.

Opinion Pieces and Comments

Is there a publication that you love to read and that you feel you have something relevant to add to? It's list time...

- Make a list of media you'd love to be in
- Include editors names and contact details
- Check out previous opinion pieces to check what subjects they have used
- Call the editor and ask! Most editors are happy to have a good opinion article from an industry expert
- Consider letters to the editor. Even if your letter does not get printed, you have a great starting point for a blog or article

Journalists are often looking for comments to add to their articles. Take a note of what journalists write in your target publications and contact them with a list of the types of issues you could comment on and then how they can contact you.

Speaking and Workshops

Are you happy to stand up and talk in front of others? If you are not, is there someone else who works in your business that is happy to do this? It's a great way to get yourself and your business in front of lots of people at the same time.

A good way to start yourself off as a speaker is to attend local **networking** groups, meet people, and perhaps do some speaking there to start you off. Go networking with the intention of building long term relationships with others – you need to be in it for the long haul. Some people say networking does not work – but that's often because they go with the intention of finding business or a sale. Be a giver and be organised.

I always plan who I want to speak to before a networking event. Follow up with people straight away and book 1:1s so that you can get to know other people's businesses properly.

You never know where business will come from. Word of mouth is still the best PR and networking is a great way to start this off.

If you are going to have a go at some **speaking** then make sure you practice with a small audience, it's also worth getting a coach to run through your talk with you. I've found this really helpful in the past.

Practice with any audio-visual and make sure everything is working properly. If you can get your talk videoed then that can be useful for your own social media.

If standing up on your own in front of an audience fills you with dread then consider whether putting on a **workshop** might be beneficial. You could join with another business person and run one together. Make sure you both have similar clients and that you can work together with ease. Practice.

 **Awards**

There are so many awards around that you can enter as a business or business person. Have a look at local ones as well as industry specific ones.

- Check the categories and make sure you are eligible before you enter

- Gather all the information you will need for the application – you may need company financial information and testimonials

- Have something lined up for additional information such as a video and some blog posts you have written (judging can get tedious so it helps to have something interesting lined up!)

- Follow the awards on social media and give them some love – even if you don't get nominated you will gain some new followers

- If you do get nominated, make the most of it. Get some interviews lined up, attend the awards (or send a representative who can collect on your behalf) and make the most of the chance to network with some new people

- If you win that is wonderful, but even if you don't it is always worth the effort of entering

How brand ambassadors can help you

First of all let's start with who a brand ambassador (a.k.a influencer) is.

Your biggest fan.

Someone who will "big up" your business and brand. There are 3 types

- A **genuine** user of your product who spreads the joy of your company via word of mouth, social media and blogs.

- An employee who is loyal, totally involved in the business and the brand and shares love.

- You, the business owner. 24/7 you represent your brand.

Why do you need one?

Word of mouth is a brilliant and effective PR.

A brand ambassador who genuinely loves your brand is a fantastic promotional tool for your business. They will speak positively about you and your business to many people.

Others will often be more likely to believe someone else who speaks about you than your own advertising or marketing collateral – but only if the relationship is genuine.

Who makes a good ambassador and where do I find one?

Ask your customers who are loyal if they want the opportunity to help your brand. You will need to give them something in return – a discount or free product.

Keep an eye on your social media and see who mentions you or is active daily.

Brand Ambassadors do not need to be a famous person – but they do need to be good customers and active socially.

Bloggers can make excellent ambassadors, but again, I do want to reiterate how important it is that they genuinely like your product or brand. It's wonderful if someone well-known wants to support your brand but the public are wise to a non – genuine promotion.

In some companies, you may not be able to use customers or their stories but the people who work for you or are part of the company can be excellent ambassadors.

Help your employees to become involved in the brand – share their stories, share their accomplishments and their hobbies or charity fundraising.

I advise you make sure you have an agreement in writing between yourself and your ambassador that details what free products/ discounts you will offer them and how much you require in return. Make sure this is detailed and the ambassador is aware of how often you expect social media mentions, whether you want to use their photo or expect them to wear your logo on occasions. It helps give your ambassador a script that they can use when they speak to people or when they are on social media; it's important that they reflect the tone of voice of your company and brand.

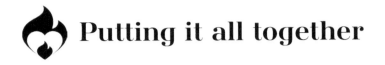 Putting it all together

Monitoring results

Digital Media and Social Media is easy to monitor and there are increasingly better tools available that both pick up coverage and monitor the results of it. You can get measurements for aspects such as reach, engagement, number of shares, number of links and value.

As a PR company we have media monitoring that picks up digital, broadcast and print as well as social shares. We can then produce some detailed reports for our clients. You should always know exactly what response you are getting to all of your promotion.

And remember...
Everything you say and do is PR

I'm sure my clients get fed up about me banging on about this but everything you say and do is PR.

You never know who you are going to meet by chance.

Be ready!

 # Useful Stuff

PR Checklist… A quick recap:

- Who are your customers and who do you want to be your customers?

- What do they read and watch and what are they interested in?

- What communication tools do you currently use to reach current and potential customers?

- What else could you add into the mix?

- Decide exactly what you want to promote first

- Make sure it's (product or service) easy to buy – do you have stock? Is the buying process easy?

- Make a list of the channels you are going to use to promote it

- Prioritise what you will do first and work together with marketing and social media to make sure the campaign is integrated

- Staff training. Make sure everyone in your company is aware of what you are promoting and why and knows how to speak about your product and service

- Consider media training for staff and brand ambassadors who may get interviewed

 The Bit About Me

When I was a kid I wanted to be a famous horse rider. The ambition took over my life day in and day out. I was sensible enough to realise that I might need a career to pay for the horses, so I worked hard at school as well as at my riding and ended up at Bristol University. During Uni, I worked every weekend at a professional riders' yard, getting up at 5am to drive there in my knackered old Talbot. It was something my Uni friends couldn't understand – I sometimes admit I went to work having not been to bed – but it was the only way I could keep up my riding and my training.

After Uni, I spent 3 years working on the yards of Olympic and professional riders, learning everything I could. I'd managed to get a couple of horses of my own by then and when the money got tight I took a part-time lecturing job at Wiltshire College. During this time I found I had a way of getting along with all sorts of difficult horses that others struggled with, I worked out how to make them more manageable and how to get them working with me. It didn't take me too long to realise that I could do this with people too.

I found the college job tough, as a free spirit there were rather too many rules for my liking. In 2005, I saw a job advertised for one of my favourite brands, the clothing brand of Olympic champion Anky Van Grunsven. It was a sales job but with the UK marketing and PR as well. This was when I first met Monique Van Dooren-Westerdaal who is still a huge influence in my life. I was OK at sales, not brilliant, but I learned. What I did discover was that I was good at the strategy for the brand and foreseeing the possibilities and connections we needed. I set out to learn everything I could about PR, marketing and strategy. At this point I was still riding at as many national shows as possible, often on other riders' cast off horses. I was never going to be world champion but I competed against the best and trained with the best. I learned what it takes to get to the very top of a sport or a profession and this learning has become part of the difference I can make with my clients.

Now retired personally from equestrian sport, but a keen runner, I am constantly using the things I learned from my time in sport, in business.

The Thank-You Bit

Firstly I have to say thanks to my family for bearing with me – I fully admit to being extremely focussed (they would probably say obsessive) over my business and my clients.

I wouldn't be doing what I am now if it wasn't for Monique Van Dooren-Westerdaal and her continuous support and friendship. We still have many plans together. Watch this space.

Business-wise I need to thank Niki Matyjasik for keeping me grounded and being there on the end of the phone when I need to run stuff by her.

Gary J Keating gets a special mention for opening my eyes to a world of possibilities, and helping me be brave enough to go after them. Jane Carvell for helping me stay true to myself.

Vik Martin who encouraged me to start writing in the first place.

And to Amy Morse who made this book become a reality.

Thank you all.